This book is dedicated to my daughter, my beautiful butterfly

🦋 Azara Nalea Eve Williams 🦋

This book belongs to

Azara

The Little Princess Who Loves Dresses

January 2021
"Good Morning Mommy!"
"Good Morning Azara!"

"Can I wear a lovely dress today?"

"Azara did you brush your teeth and use the bathroom?"

"No Mommy!"

"Well, when you do those things, and finish your breakfast, you can wear one of your lovely dresses."

Azara jumps out of bed and runs to the bathroom to brush her teeth and take a bath.

"Look Mommy; I am all finished!"
"Can I have my breakfast please?"

"Sure Azara, what would you like to eat?"

Azara thought for a second, hmm...

"I would like to have chocolates."

"Chocolates?" Said Mommy with a surprised look on her face!

"Come on, Azara, it's too early for chocolates."

"Hmm, oh all right Mommy, I would like to have bread and cheese with some milk please."

"That's more like it!" "Said Mommy."

Azara finished her breakfast quickly and put her empty plate and cup in the sink;

"Good Job Azara!"

"Thank you Mommy."

"Can I please put my dress on now?"

"You sure can," said Mommy.

Azara went to her room and opened her closet door, as she gazed at her many different choices she thought, which one should I wear today?

"Would you like the white one with polka dots?"

"No Mommy!"

"What about the blue dress with stripes?"

"I don't like stripes any more Mommy."

"Do you like the purple one with little animal paintings?"

"No Mommy"

"How about the yellow one with short sleeves?"

"No Mommy, I wore that yesterday."

"Ok Azara, which one would you like to wear?"

"I like the pink one with the frills at the bottom."

"Ok then, the pink one it is! Let me help you put it on."

Azara looks at herself in the mirror with glee.

"I look like a beautiful princess!"

"You are a beautiful princess Azara."

"But always remember it is your inner beauty that matters the most."

"I love you Mommy!"

"I love you more my princess."

Azara leaves her room ready to start her day, feeling confident in her lovely pink dress.

CPSIA information can be obtained
at www.ICGtesting.com
Printed in the USA
LVHW072308220421
684848LV00025B/657

9 781777 583910